IMAGES OF \

COMBINED ROUND THE CLOCK BOMBING OFFENSIVE: ATTACKING NAZI GERMANY

RARE PHOTOGRAPHS FROM WARTIME ARCHIVES

PHILIP KAPLAN

WITH JACK CURRIE

Pen & Sword
AVIATION

First printed in Great Britain in 2015 by
Pen & Sword Aviation
an imprint of
Pen & Sword Books Ltd.
47 Church Street
Barnsley,
South Yorkshire
S70 2AS

A CIP record for this book is available from the
British Library.

ISBN 978 1 78 346 3046

Printed and bound in Malta
By Gutenberg Press Ltd

Pen & Sword Books Ltd incorporates the
Imprints of Pen & Sword Aviation, Pen & Sword
Family History, Pen & Sword Maritime, Pen &
Sword Military, Pen & Sword Discovery,
Wharncliffe Local History, Wharncliffe True
Crime, Wharncliffe Transport, Pen & Sword
Select, Pen & Sword Military Classics, Leo
Cooper, The Praetorian Press, Remember When,
Seaforth Publishing and Frontline Publishing.

For a complete list of Pen & Sword titles please
contact Pen & Sword Books Limited
47 Church Street, Barnsley, South Yorkshire, S70
2AS, England

E-mail: enquiries@pen-and-sword.co.uk
Website: www.pen-and-sword.co.uk

Contents

THE HARDWARE   3
COUNTRY FOLK   22
DINGHY, DINGHY   32
MUD AND MUSCLE   42
AIRCREW   49
A BRITISH RAID   64
DAYLIGHT RAIDERS   86
ABANDON!   102
TO THE BIG CITY   114
ROUND THE CLOCK   124
WAR PAINT   134

The author is grateful to the following for the
use of their published and/or unpublished
material, and for their kind assistance in the
preparation of this book: Fred Allen, John Archer,
Roger A. Armstrong, Beth and David Alston, Eric
Barnard, Sy Bartlett, Malcolm Bates, Mike
Benarcik, Robert Best, Ron Bicker, Larry Bird,
Quentin Bland, Charles Bosshardt, Sam Burchell,
Leonard Cheshire, Don Charlwood, Paul Chryst,
Winston Churchill, Jack Clift, John Comer, N.J.
Crisp, Jack Currie (for his text) Jim Dacey, E.W.
Deacon, James H. Doolittle, Lawrence Drew,
Spencer Dunmore, Ira Eakin, Gary Eastman,
Jonathan Falconer, W.W. Ford, Alan Foreman,
Stephen Fox, Noble Frankland, Carsten Fries,
Toni Frissell, Bill Ganz, Stephen Grey, Roland
Hammersley, Arthur Harris, Ian Hawkins, John
Hersey, Dave Hill, Franc Isla, Claire and Joe
Kaplan, Neal Kaplan, Margaret Kaplan, Paul Kemp,
Percy Kindred, Nick Kosiuk, Edith Kup, William T.
Larkins, W.J. Lawrence, Beirne Lay, Jr., Robert D.
Loomis, David C. Lustig, Donald Maffett, Dickie
Mayes, Cheryl and Mike Mathews, Edward R.
Murrow, Frank Nelson, Keith Newhouse, Michael
O'Leary, Merle Olmsted, Tony Partridge, Colin
Paterson, John Pawsey, L.W. Pilgrim, Reg Payne,
Douglas Radcliffe, Sidney Rapoport, Lynn Ray,
Duane Reed, Alan Reeves, Ted Richardson, Kay
Riley, Dave Shelhamer, Paul Sink, John Skilleter,
Dale O. Smith, Tony Starcer, James Stewart, Ken
Stone, Lloyd Stovall, John Thomas, Leonard
Thompson, Albert Tyler, Forrest Vosler, Mae
West, Robert White, Ray Wild, Joe Williams, Jack
Woods, Dennis Wrynn, Sam Young. Efforts have
been made to trace copyright holders to use
their material. The author apologizes for any
omissions. All reasonable efforts will be made to
correct any such omissions in future editions.

The bomb-aimer of an RAF
Avro Lancaster bomber.

A B-17F Flying Fortress bomber of the 91st Bomb Group on a practice mission over England.

To describe warplanes in terms of their statistics—weight, length and wingspan, bombloads and armament, power plants and cruising speeds—is for books of reference. The figures are factual and give no cause for argument. To offer an opinion on less definable characteristics—maneuverability, effectiveness, feel, or appearance—is to be subjective and to risk making hackles rise somewhere in the world; to compare like with like—the B-17, say, with the B-24, the Lancaster with the Halifax, the Spitfire with the Hurricane, or the P-47 with the P-51—and to state that either airplane was superior, is to court an argument with the other's champions.

Veterans of the air war have it in common that they had, and had to have, faith in their aircraft; that was the plane that saw them through their missions: they will regard it with affection and guard its reputation evermore. The opinions, therefore, that follow in this chapter should be read with that loyalty in mind.

There was a time after graduation when Ray Wild's ambition was to fly a pursuit plane. "But a little major got up and asked if any of us red-blooded Americans wanted to get into action right now. We raised our hands, and they sent us to Sebring, Florida, on B-17s. We knew nothing about them. They looked like great big lumbering things, and we weren't too happy, really. They used to send you to gunnery range, for the waist and tail gunners to shoot at targets, and you realized it was steady—a great platform to shoot from. We started to like the airplane. That thing could be ten feet off the ground and hold steady. You put it on automatic pilot and it held steady. You didn't do it, of course, but you could.

"Now, the B-24 was ten miles an hour faster, it cruised at 170, but it had a Davis wing, which was a great wing, except that if you got hit in one wing that doubled the stress on the other. It could get hit lightly and go down. A B-17, you could chop in little pieces and that sonofabitch would come back. It would fly when it shouldn't fly. We lost eight feet of wing one time and twelve feet off the stabilizer, and it handled the same way. A little sluggish, maybe, but it was fine. You could lose two engines on one side in a 17 and so long as you turned into the live engines, you could fly it. Everybody knew that the plane would get back. If they could stay in it and stay alive, they knew they'd get back. The only way you wouldn't was with a direct hit or with a wing blown off. You got a great affinity with it. Of course, the B-24 pilots said the same thing. For them the 24 was the best airplane in the world."

For an aircraft designed in 1934 as the very first all-metal four-engined monoplane bomber, the "Fort" had a marvelous career. Don Maffett realized its robust qualities on the first of his forty missions with the 452nd Bomb Group. "The left wheel was shot off, but I didn't know that, and I landed on one wheel. The airplane had three-hundred-and-fifty flak holes in it. The B-17 could take a lot of punishment—I think far more than the B-24. Shot up or in good shape, the B-17 was pretty consistent. You'd come in over the fence at a hundred-and-ten miles an hour and it would stall out at ninety-two or ninety-three. It gave you a tremendous feeling of confidence."

There used to be a tale that when a prototype bomber was wheeled out of the factory, you would see a group of men with slide rules walking anxiously around it. The answer to the question as to who those men might be, and what they were about, was that they were the designers, trying to find a place to put the crew. Don Maffett, for one, had some reservations about the pilot's compartment in the B-17: "It was very cramped. There was very little

below: Its hydraulics shot out during a raid, this Boeing B-17G was able to make a successful belly-landing at its Bassingbourn, England, base in 1944; bottom left: Air Chief Marshal Arthur Harris, headed RAF Bomber Command in WW2; bottom right: Lt. General Jimmy Doolittle commanded the Eighth USAAF from January 1944.

Top left: The pilot of an 8AF Flying Fortress; left: Major Pierce McKennon who led the 335th Fighter Squadron of the 4th Fighter Group, 8AF, from their Debden, Essex base in 1944-45.

above: B-17s of the 390th
Bomb Group attacking an
aircraft plant at Marienburg,
Germany, 9 October 1943.

"There was always a controversy about the B-17 and the B-24," said Paul Sink. "I flew in them both and I always thought the B-17 was the better airplane. It was a very good aircraft. But the B-24 was a good aircraft too." So it was: with its great endurance and bomb bay capacity, it was effective in the Pacific theater, and as a U-boat destroyer it was the RAF Coastal Command's most successful aircraft.

Frank Nelson was another flier who had operational experience of both aircraft. In July 1944, he was midway through his tour as a navigator on B-24s when his group—the 487th at Lavenham in Suffolk—reequipped with B-17s. Nelson was glad of that, because "in the B-17s we could get up to over twenty-thousand feet, and this made quite a difference as far as flak was concerned. Also it ran our true airspeed up to two-hundred knots or a little better, which meant we were out of the flak that much quicker."

W.W. Ford agreed with Nelson's view. "The 24s couldn't hold the altitude the 17s could hold. The flak was heavier down at their altitude and the fighters would pick on them before us, because usually the P-51s were above us in more strength than they were around the 24s. They got clobbered a lot worse than we did." Ford, however, did remember one elderly B-17 at Podington of which it was rumoured that, if anybody pulled a certain cotter key in the bomb bay, the whole airplane would disintegrate. "I could believe it," said Ford. "That B-17 always sounded like it was gonna fall apart."

In the same way that the early Halifaxes had to bomb below the Lancasters, the B-24s usually operated several thousand feet below the B-17s. At 20,000 feet, the B-24 became too unstable to fly in close formation, and its slow rate of ascent gave rise to other problems, as Keith Newhouse found when he took off from Rackheath in *Wallowing Wilbur* in late April 1944, and began a long climb through the overcast. At 12,000 feet ice was building up on all the frontal surfaces and, a few moments later, *Wallowing Wilbur* stalled. Newhouse regained control, the co-pilot opened the throttles and lowered a little flap to give the airfoils more lift, but the ice continued to accrete. The port wing went down, and the aircraft lost two-thousand feet of altitude. Twice more, Newhouse tried to climb above the icing level, and each time was frustrated. By then, the airplane had taken on so much ice that he could not maintain height, let alone increase it. He turned back to Rackheath and, shortly afterward, the force was instructed by radio to abandon the mission.

Early in his tour with 44 Squadron at Waddington, Laurence Pilgrim was en route to Duisburg in the Ruhr, when an airplane below him exploded and turned his Lancaster upside down. Aerobatics in a fully-laden bomber were to be avoided, especially in the dark and with the gyro instruments toppled, but Pilgrim had no choice: he had either to roll out with ailerons and rudders, or pull the stick back as in the last half of a loop. Ordering his flight engineer to reduce the power, Pilgrim chose the half-loop as the less unpleasant prospect. The engineer, as it happened, was lying on the cabin roof; falling into place, he knocked the throttles back—exactly at the moment when Pilgrim, recovering, wanted them wide open. Having got their act together, the crew flew on to Duisburg. Since that occurrence, Pilgrim maintained that the Lancaster was fully aerobatic.

A few months later, a 12 Squadron pilot had an experience that was, if anything, even more alarming. On the last of the Hamburg firestorm raids in Operation Gomorrah, the approach to the target was barred by towering thunderclouds, one of which he entered while avoiding flak. Instantly, the Lancaster was covered in a heavy layer of ice; the controls

left: A still from the Associated British Pictures Corporation film *The Dam Busters*, with Richard Todd and Robert Shaw, released in 1954; below: Repair work under way on a Handley Page Halifax bomber in November 1942.

left: A Lancaster powered by American Packard-Merlin engines; right: The elegant de Havilland Mosquito fighter-bomber; below: Factory assembly of a Short Stirling bomber; bottom right: Examining flak damage to a Stirling.

picked up A.A. Milne's *When We Were Very Young* and *Now We Are Six*. The two of us laughed and chuckled all the way home swapping the stories back and forth.

"Sunday, April 16. Trees are popping buds, flowers are in bloom and fruit trees are all a-blossom. It is lovely and growing more so. The thing that forces itself on the observer here is the system of fences. They appear in all forms, sizes, and lengths. Every little plot has its perimeter defined by some manner of pickets, lathes, wire, stone wall or shrubbery—anything to form a dividing line. A Westerner would feel he had been set down in somebody's idea of what a child's world should be like. The whole scene gives a rather cozy feeling.

"Saturday, May 13. The London leave was perfect. The number of cabs and the crowds on the street impressed us at first. I've never seen as many cabs, even in Chicago. We never had any trouble getting one, and they were cheap until blackout time. Then the sky was the limit. A trip that cost about thirty cents in daylight ran about $1 after dark. We didn't have much trouble getting a hotel room and had excellent food in one of the officers' clubs. We bought some clothes down at the big PX and then went in search of liquor. We finally bought Booth's dry gin and some good scotch at $13 a fifth for the gin and $17 for the whiskey. So, for about $50 we managed to get stinking enough not to be interested in the stuff next day, and to go to *Something For The Boys* the following evening. It was a fair show, but the chorus saved the day. What seductive legs, and, of course, we were only three rows from the front.

"We traveled to Lou's field by train. Their cars are called coaches and are about half the length of ours. Six people sit in a nice first class compartment. The seats are feather-soft, with arm-rests, and the upholstery is a delicate, flowery broadcloth sort of weave. The toilets are twice the size of American train closets and kept spic-and-span. For the most part, our travel back to home was in the top of a double-decker bus. We had box seats for the lovely panorama that is the English countryside. This island is beautiful."

"I've heard a lot of bad remarks," said Ira Eakin, "about the English people, but don't believe it. They're great in my book. They really treated us great. They would come around those bases every weekend and invite so many GIs to their homes, and a lot of times they'd take you out there and fix you a good meal, and they were doing without themselves, we found out later." Paul Sink agreed: "The English made a lot of sacrifices for the Americans there in World War Two."

Most men in their twenties are mentally resilient: they adapt readily to change. Even so, the bomber crews couldn't fail to notice the extraordinary contrast between their operational environment and their free time on the ground. "The unusual thing was," Jack Clift remarked, "you'd be on ops one night and at a party the next night. You'd think, It's unreal, this. There we were, up dicing with death last night and here we are at The Horse and Jockey, living it up. It was very strange."

She walks in beauty like the night / Of cloudless climes and starry skies; / And all that's best of dark and bright / Meet in her aspect and her eyes: Thus mellowed to that tender light Which Heaven to gaudy day denies.
—from *She Walks in Beauty* by Lord Byron

Love is an ocean of emotions,entirely surrounded by expenses.
—Lord Dewar

Tonight our orders are: 'Bomb the centre of Bremen; make it uninhabitable for the workers.' England! Cricket! Huh! Justifiable? I do not know. I only know that I shall kill women and children soon.
—from *Journeys Into Night* by Don Charlwood

Mrs Kirby's weekly food ration comprised four ounces of bacon; two ounces of butter plus four ounces of margarine or lard; two ounces of tea; eight ounces of sugar; one shilling and tuppence worth of meat, which amounted to about thirteen ounces or less, depending on price; and a cheese ration which varied considerably during the war, but averaged around two or three ounces a week. In addition she was entitled to one egg; one packet of dried eggs; eight ounces of jam; and twelve ounces of chocolate or sweets. Milk was 'controlled' at around two or two and a half pints per person per week. Potatoes, bread and fresh vegetables were not rationed, but the latter were scarce and distributed on a controlled basis. Tinned and packet foods were on 'points'. Mrs Kirby was entitled to twenty points per four week period. One packet of breakfast cereal, one tin of pilchards, half a pound of chocolate biscuits, one pound of rice, and one tin of grade three salmon, added up to twenty points, and so, Mrs Kirby's entitlement for a whole month. At twenty-four points for a one-pound tin, stewed steak was a luxury available only to housewives with several ration books at their disposal. For a nation of tea drinkers, the meagre ration of two ounces a week was probably the greatest hardship.

Otherwise, the draconian rationing system equalized hunger, as it were; no one starved, and the health of the British people actually improved, which said much about the pre-war British diet, inequalities and deprivations of the unemployed and the poorly paid.
—from *Yesterday's Gone* by N.J. Crisp

Man has his will—but woman has her way.
—from *The Autocrat of the Breakfast Table* by Oliver Wendell Holmes

A still from the Columbia Pictures film *The War Lover*, adapted from the novel by John Hersey. The 1962 film starred Steve McQueen, Robert Wagner, and Shirley Ann Field.

Dinghy, Dinghy, Prepare To Ditch

Ambulance crewmen awaiting the return of the group aircraft from the day's mission to Germany.

Just how many warplanes ditched in the waters between England and Europe while return-
ing from their missions will never be accurately known, but of the airmen who were reported to have ditched, or whose last distress messages were received by radio, it is certain that
the majority survived. This was largely due to the efforts of the Air-Sea Rescue Service, joint-
ly controlled by the RAF and the Royal Navy, and tasked with saving airmen of the Allied
forces (and sometimes of the Luftwaffe) from the perils of the sea.

The first sea rescue of an American bomber crew in World War Two was effected on 2
October 1942, after the Eighth Air Force's "first real brawl" over Lille. Two damaged B-17s
had gone down in the English Channel, and what follows is the story of one whose crew was
saved. "The fun began," the pilot stated, "as we started home. We got plenty of flak, and we
were under attack from fighters. A Focke-Wulf 190 winged us with a cannon shell, and the
outer starboard engine started smoking quite badly. The generators were knocked out and
the intercom went dead."

There was probably more damage than the crew were aware of, for the aircraft lost altitude at fifteen hundred feet a minute. As every wartime airman knew, the Channel was the
shortest stretch of water in the world on the outbound route, and the longest coming back.
The pilot decided that, on this occasion, it was going to be too long. It so happened that his
crew had practiced ditching drills the day before the mission, but then they had been able
to use the intercom; now, when it mattered, communication had to be by word of mouth.

Five thousand feet above the water, the pilot handed over to the co-pilot and went aft.
To lighten the aircraft, he had the waist guns jettisoned, and instructed the gunners to assemble in the radio compartment; the navigator and the bombardier were told to join them
from the nose. "Then I went back to the controls," said the pilot, "and got ready to ditch the
ship. We removed our parachutes and adjusted our Mae Wests. The water looked cold, and
it also looked hard."

There had never been such a thing as a practice ditching. You could rehearse the drill for
taking up position in the aircraft, bracing for the impact, and finding the cables that released
the dinghies; in the local swimming pools, you could practice inflating the Mae West, handling
the dinghy, and trying to climb aboard; but the only time a pilot set an airplane down on
water was when there was no other option . As to how it should be done, instructions in
the manuals tended to be sparse. They suggested it was best to lower a little flap and touch
down with the airplane in a level attitude; there was a further—if unwritten—school of
thought that advocated ditching along the swell rather than across it; but no pilot could be
blamed, in the stresses of the moment, if he failed to bear all those all those maxims in his
mind. The Flying Fortress pilot did his best.

"We laid her down," he said, "in a belly landing as slowly as we could, with the tail well
down. There were waves, and I had heard that when you hit a wave the effect is very much
like flying into a stone wall. It was. We hit so hard that it threw the crew all over the ship."

Two men were knocked unconscious, and the others were momentarily dazed. Coming
to their senses, they tried to launch the dinghies, of which two had been so damaged as to
be unseaworthy; the third could be only partially inflated. "Then came another problem," the
pilot continued. "When the men started dropping into the water, they realized that the win-
ter equipment some of them were wearing was too heavy for their Mae Wests to support.
Splashing around in the icy water, those in lighter clothing managed to hold the others up

35

Smith did something. Digging in the mire on one of the base roads, he came to solid concrete, and set every man to work with spades and shovels. "There were miles of roads, but we had thousands of people. They grumbled, but they shoveled, and the roads began to clear. I put out an order that trucks were to stay on the pavement and pass only at the concrete turnouts."

After one sergeant truck driver had been busted to private on the spot, there were no more offenders. Morale seemed to improve, men could ride on bicycles and walk without overshoes. Then Smith discovered that a fleet of mud-caked dump trucks were engaged in moving massive piles of earth from one site to another on the base, and undoing all the efforts of the last two weeks.

"The mud movers," Smith recorded, "were working for the Duke of Buccleuch, who owned the base. I tried the phone but the Duke was shooting in Scotland. I requested his manager to stop the trucks but he said he could do nothing without the Duke's approval. I instructed my ground exec. to put guards on the gates to those mud fields and not let a single truck pass. All hell broke loose. High-ranking Brits from the Air Ministry called me: the Duke was a member of the Royal family. Generals from Eighth Air Force headquarters admonished me: the rental agreement allowed the Duke to use our roads, I was injuring relations with our allies, etc."

The colonel stood firm: no more ducal trucks while he was in command. Daily, he expected transfer orders to arrive. None did. The trucks and the power shovel stayed immobile in the fields, and were still there eleven months later when he left Grafton Underwood—no longer under mud.

"That weather!" exclaimed Ira Eakin. "I asked a lot of English people and they said it wasn't like that before the war started. All those explosives going off and all that kinda stuff. But the three years that I was there, you could take all the sunshine and bunch it up and you wouldn't have made a month of it. It was unbelievable. We'd take off from Bassingbourn and you could see for miles, and you wouldn't be up there five minutes and you couldn't see nowhere. You'd just keep on climbing till you climbed out of that stuff. You might come back and it would be clear. But it was raining, foggy, snowing—something—most of the time."

Throughout his tour with the 92nd Bomb Group at Podington, Ray Wild called every B-17 he flew *Mizpah* (Hebrew, meaning "May God protect us while we are apart from one another."), although the name was only ever painted on the first. After that original *Mizpah*, he flew a total of nine different aircraft. "If you got one shot up, maybe they'd repair it or use it for spare parts, and the next day you'd be flying a different airplane. It could have flown ninety-two missions, or this could have been its first, but the ground crews were so great, it didn't make much difference."

Larry Bird was always grateful to the men who tended the aircraft of the 493rd Bomb Group at Debach. "Most of those guys," he said, "were off the farm two years before, but we wouldn't be here now if it wasn't for them and the conscientious way they worked. They would start on those airplanes whatever time you came in and work on them continuously until you took off next morning on a mission. They never stopped. I've seen guys work at night with a flashlight in their mouths so they could have both hands free. Cold as hell, raining, foggy. I know I really feel warm about those guys."

One of those guys was armourer Sam Burchell of the 448th Bomb Group at Seething:

"In the evening, there'd be a message from the top sergeant when to start loading, and we'd go to our particular planes and put the bombs on—fragmentation, five-hundred-pounders or whatever. That generally took from eleven at night to four or five in the morning. When the planes left, we'd go and have breakfast and then sleep till noon or so. The fifty-caliber guns tended to jam on occasion, which could be from the cold, and there were problems with the hydraulically operated turrets, but nothing spectacular. I wasn't that much of a mechanic, but the guys who were a little older had been working in gas stations and that, and they could fix those things."

However careful and skillful the armourers might be, there was always the danger of a "hang-up" in the air. In the Lancaster and Halifax, with their capacious bomb bays, this was seldom more than an inconvenience: the offending bomb could usually be shaken off, or released when the aircraft was at a lower, warmer altitude. In the narrow bomb bay of a Fortress, however, where the bombs were stacked one upon another, it could be more embarrassing. Half Larry Bird's load of five-hundred-pounders, on one such occasion, were logjammed by a lower, hung-up bomb. Armed with a screwdriver and a relay of portable oxygen bottles, he set out to resolve the situation. "I bet I was down there twenty-five or thirty minutes," he recalled, "on this little catwalk just inches wide, with the bomb doors open, trying to get that thing away, and the longer I was down there, the madder I got. There wasn't enough room to wear a parachute, and the airplane was really bouncing around. Those bombs were charged and ready to explode. There was a lot of drag on the airplane with the bomb doors being open, and the pilot was struggling to stay with the formation. He kept sending messages back, like 'Get on with it, Bird, dammit!' I was working like the devil and it

left: A coffee and doughnuts wagon on an airfield of the Eighth; below: At war with the ever-present mud of an American air base in World War Two England.

was really cold. Finally, I got that shackle to release, and they all went. It just so happened we were passing over the American lines, but I didn't know that at the time."

The squadron was based at Ludford Magna, northeast of Lincoln. It was a pretty soggy spot. We called it Mudford Stagna.
—Pete Johnson, pilot, 101 Squadron, Royal Air Force

The rain slanted under the wing on a raw northeast wind. Of Cambridgeshire we had only an impression screened through the deluge—somber flatness, and mud; mud oozing up over the edge of the asphalt circle where we were parked; mud in the tread of the jeep, which rolled away on twin tracks of ochre, leaving us marooned; a vast plain, or lake of mud stretching off toward a cluster of barely visible buildings.
—from *The War Lover* by John Hersey

The stars were out that night. I liked that very much because it meant a hard freeze and out of the mud for at least two or three days. Also, it sent a message to the combat crews: get ready for a mission in the morning. With that in mind I set out my mission clothes and equipment. Most combat men developed superstitions about clothes or some special talisman they always carried on a raid. I remember one gunner who wore the same coveralls each trip and refused to have them washed. Somehow the unwashed coveralls had become his security blanket.
—from *Combat Crew* by John Comer

If there comes a little thaw, / Still the air is chill and raw, / Here and there a patch of snow, Dirtier than the ground below, / Dribbles down a marshy flood; Ankle-deep you stick in mud In the meadows while you sing, / "This is Spring."
—*A Spring Growl* by C.P. Cranch

We had bicycles to get around the base, but the mud was so bad we mostly had to carry them.
—Sam Young, bombardier, 452nd Bomb Group, Eighth U.S. Army Air Force

Talk about flying blind. It took me about ten minutes to do a one-minute walk over to the Admin block, feeling my way along the asphalt path with those heavy sloggers. I'd get off in the mud once in a while—though actually it was less soupy than usual, as we had had five days of good weather—and then feel my way back onto the hardtop; and poking along that way I got there.
—from *The War Lover* by John Hersey

Aircrew

In World War Two, the most effective fighting units were usually small—submarine crews, infantry platoons, commandos, and bomber crews. Of these, it could be said that the men who crewed the bombers caused more damage to the enemy and had a greater impact on the outcome of the conflict than any number of the rest. Most of the aircrews were volunteers (in the RAF, they all were), intelligent, fit, and highly trained. Each knew he was essential to the team, whether one of nine or ten in a Fortress or a Liberator, or one of seven in a British bomber; he knew that a mistake by any one could mean the death of all. Their interdependence was a welding influence.

When a man was trained in the USAAF to become a pilot, a navigator, or a bombardier, his training as an officer proceeded hand in hand with his training as a flier: if he flunked in either aspect he didn't graduate. It followed that those members of the crew, including the co-pilot in an Eighth Air Force bomber, were commissioned officers, while the gunners were enlisted men with the rank of sergeant. In the RAF, it was different, and many crews were entirely composed of NCOs, while some were of mixed ranks, with the pilot, of whatever rank, always being the captain of the aircraft.

"It was really a matter of luck," said Laurence Pilgrim of the RAF, "whether you got a good crew or not to start with. Once they were formed, it was up to the captain to mold them into the sort of crew he wanted. In my opinion, if the crew didn't turn out well, it was the captain's fault. It was essential to go out together quite often, to have a drink together and to be as friendly as possible. Of course, the pilot had to have the crew's respect—not as NCOs to officer, but as crew to captain—so that if he said something in the air, they did it without question."

Dave Shelhamer of the 303rd Bomb Group also saw a need for a modicum of discipline: "I made a statement that if anybody on this crew fouls up, and it was some little thing, admonition and that would be it. But anything serious, and that person would be off the crew. Now, whether they believed I would do that, I don't know. But when Keaton really pulled a lulu and I summarily removed him from the crew, it was a kind of shock to them. After that I had a crew that worked like a well-oiled machine. They were just beautiful."

A typical RAF all-NCO crew was that of Alan Forman, who flew thirteen operations with 103 Squadron in the final stages of the war. Forman was the son of a Lincolnshire farmhand, and he had never expected to be a bomber captain. "I put in for air gunner, but there was an old First War flier, an air commodore, on the selection board, and he told me I ought to try for pilot. I told him I left school at fourteen and my maths was pretty poor, but he said not to worry about that. I was very lucky. I passed the course in Canada, while a lot of people failed. They ended up as navigators or bomb-aimers. I went through operational training and got my own crew: a Scotsman, two Yorkshiremen, three Australians, and me. Apart from the gunners, they'd all been to better schools than I had, yet there I was, twenty-one years old, commanding a crew in which the navigator was an old Etonian and the rear gunner had already done a tour of ops and had a Distinguished Flying Medal. The war was a great leveler."

From the beginning of 1943, the RAF replaced the co-pilot in its four-engined bombers with a new flight engineer, who managed the fuel system, assisted the pilot with the engine handling, and generally acted as Mister Fix-it in the air. In the USAAF, however, the co-pilot was always an integral member of the crew, with the added task, in lead planes, of checking

A young B-24 Liberator
bomber pilot in England.

from the tail turret while the lead pilot occupied his right-hand cabin seat.

Bill Ganz, who flew thirty-two missions with the 398th Bomb Group, was fully qualified to fly the B-17 but, in his time at Nuthampstead, he seldom got the chance to make a take-off or a landing: "My pilot always wanted the takeoff. I read out the checklist and made sure he went through the standard operating procedures. It was the same with the landing. Once we got off, either he or I would fly to altitude while the other watched the instruments and after formed up, we would split the formation time. That was the most tiring thing of all—

Our bombers were disposed to take advantage of the usual P-47 tactics of sweeping over us in a column of squadrons at two- or three-minute intervals, furnishing what was known as corridor support. In other words, we expected all three squadrons to keep weaving back and forth over us in turn, and to jump German formations that came up. But after two or three passes overhead . . . the P-47 squadrons pulled away and flew on to the forward task force of bombers and did not return. I was sure from this that there must be heavy going ahead, and at the same time I became apprehensive about our own situation, because I knew the Germans' habit of pouncing on unescorted formations.
—from *The War Lover* by John Hersey

flying formation."

The standard British bomber crew included two air gunners—one for the rear turret and one for the mid-upper—who (unlike their USAAF counterparts) received special training in deflection shooting air-to-air. Wireless operators were also trained in gunnery, and could replace an injured man in either turret if required. The front gun turret was seldom used on

normal operations—it was manned by the bomb-aimer on those rare occasions—and many pilots thought it served only to supplement the aircraft's "built-in head wind."

Eighth Air Force gunners, of whom there might be six or seven in a crew, often had a dual role, doubling as engineer, armorer, radio operator, or "toggleer"—a designation which entered the vocabulary when the Eighth developed the technique of formation bombing to

Members of a B-17 bomber crew, clockwise from below: top-turret gunner/flight engineer, ball turret gunner, left waist gunner, navigator, and bombardier.

above: B-17 radio operator; above right: Right waist gunner; below: In a rare instance of twins serving in the same crew, a tail gunner and his gunner brother.

a point where trained bombardiers were only needed in the lead and deputy lead crews. In an emergency, any man except the pilot might be required to fire a gun.

The rapidity with which a newly graduated USAAF bomber pilot reached a bomber squadron contrasted sharply with the progress of his British counterpart. The American could occupy the seat of a B-17 or B-24 within weeks of being awarded his pair of silver wings; the RAF man, on the other hand, after graduation underwent further courses on twin-engine aircraft before he ever got to fly a Lancaster or Halifax. There was certainly a need for overseas-trained pilots to become adjusted to the weather, the blackout, and the enemy's proximity, but 180 flying hours spread across six months seemed more than enough, certainly for those who had been trained in America. Perhaps the British air staff had not fully realized how much more air experience the USAAF Arnold Scheme provided than the Empire schools.

"Honest John" Searby was the second-tour commander of an elite RAF pathfinder squadron and a master bomber. He took the view that Bomber Command stood or fell by the quality of its navigators. "A competent, confident navigator," he wrote, "was a powerful factor for morale. Courage, determination, and the will to press on in the face of flak and fighters was one thing, but only the skill of the navigator could ensure that the effort was taken to the vital spot. So much depended on him, yet we all took him for granted. He was expected to produce the answers at the drop of a hat."

At the age of twenty-one, navigator W.W. Ford of the 92nd Bomb Group was the fourth oldest member of his crew. "The engineer was twenty-six," he recalled, "the co-pilot twenty-five, and the armorer-gunner twenty-three. The aircraft commander was the youngest—he was all of nineteen—and the rest were between nineteen and twenty. We had all denominations. The pilot was a staunch bluestocking Presbyterian, we had a Jewish boy from Brooklyn, one gunner was a Mormon, the engineer was a southern Baptist, I think the tail gunner was a Methodist, the radio operator and one of the waist gunners were Catholics, the other waist gunner was a Protestant, and I was in the Episcopal church. As for the co-pilot, I'm sure he was at least an agnostic."

In May 1944, Keith Newhouse, by then a deputy lead pilot with the 790th Bomb Squadron, made this diary note: "We flew a practice mission and took along the navigator who has just been assigned to us. He is not operational yet, and is as green as England's rolling hills. Had him lost any number of times. It was only his second trip in a B-24, and his first time at altitude. He has lots to learn."

Navigator Sidney Rapoport arrived in England in the late summer of 1944 and was at once required to undertake a radar course. "The first thing at Alconbury," he said, "was indoctrination—you had to forget whatever you had learned about navigation in the States. We started from scratch and it was a crash program." Discovering a talent for operating Mickey, Rapoport passed the course with flying colours and was assigned to the 94th Bomb Group at Bury St Edmunds, where he joined a pathfinder crew of the 333rd Squadron. At first he flew practice missions every day. "We went up to 25,000 feet and made a lot of bomb runs—the library in Cambridge, Oxford University, and many other points. British radar was checking us and giving us the score. Then we would fly a mission and get a seventy-two-hour pass. That was a marvelous privilege."

Fred Allen's Halifax crew was formed during training in the customary RAF do-it-yourself

The crew of Bruce Buckham prior to boarding their Lancaster at Waddington.

way. "There were probably three hundred in the room, and you don't know who's who. You just start walking about and if you liked the look of someone: 'Have you got a gunner?' The pilot was six foot three and I thought, he can handle anything. We hit it off and that was that. Then me and another gunner talked and I said, 'I'll go in the tail if you like.' He said, 'That suits me, I'll go in the mid-upper.' We picked the engineer up at heavy conversion unit. At thirty-eight, he was an old man, nearly twice our age. But he knew engines, plus he played piano and he had an accordion. He was always useful and a good man with the crew."

In common with every crew who cared about survival, Allen's crewmates in *Friday The Thirteenth* were sparing in their use of the intercom. "We wouldn't say a word that wasn't absolutely necessary. We had a spare bod on board once, and he kept thinking his intercom was bust because he couldn't hear anything. He said afterward he'd never flown with a crew that were so quiet. We thought if we kept the intercom clear, it would be there when we needed it. You didn't want to have to say 'Oy, get off the intercom, this is important.' Too late then. Fractions of seconds counted. Maybe that's why we did thirty-eight ops and always came back."

Paul Sink of the 93rd confirmed Fred Allen's view. "Usually in the airplane, it was very quiet: the only time we had much conversation was while we were under attack, calling out positions, type of aircraft, losses, or whatever. For the rest of the time the intercom was kept very clear."

With two engines giving trouble, Allen's crew once landed at a USAAF base, and he chatted with the Fortress gunners. "We wouldn't go up at night," they told him, "don't know how you can do it." Allen examined the B-17's ball turret with interest. "The gunner was a bit tight in there," he commented. "He needed somebody to help him out. We saw them come back from a trip next day and one of those ball turrets was shot away underneath. There was half a body in it. And they couldn't understand us going at night."

Although in Air Force circles the ball turret was referred to as "the morgue," statistics show that the occupant's chances of survival were slightly better than the other gunners'. For his part, Ken Stone of the 381st was content with the position: "I could turn through 360 degrees, I could go down, turn around, and go back up, so I had vision all the way around the plane. I could see everything."

Comparing it, however, with the isolation of the ball and tail positions, and with the numbing chill of the waist positions, Larry Bird favoured the toggleer's location: "There was a hot air vent in the nose, and I didn't need to wear an electric suit or any of that stuff. Sitting there in the nose, you had one of the most beautiful views in the world—the Swiss Alps, Lake Constance—I was in a very good spot. I didn't have to worry about the bombsight: my job was to handle that little button and keep my eye on the lead plane. As soon as I saw his bomb doors open, I'd open mine. Everybody opens in unison. So when the bombs go, they go together, and they make a pattern of explosions on the ground, same shape as the formation."

Navigator Charles Bosshardt recalled that a nose gunner's station in the B-24 was not always a healthy place to be: "We lost the hydraulics to the nose, the turret whipped around, and the doors blew off. Ernie Devries was in there holding on for dear life to keep from getting sucked out. He was a cotton-topped kid from Roberts, Montana, about eighteen years old, and he used to call me Pa. Finally he made his plight known to me, and I used the manual

crank so he could get out. After that, he felt even closer to me."

It wasn't every man who had the mental stamina to go on, mission after mission, knowing that the odds against survival were getting longer all the time. Sometimes, resolution failed, and that was not surprising. The remarkable thing was that so few combat fliers ever threw in the towel. One RAF pilot who flew a tour of operations at a time when Bomber Command's losses were at their worst, said of such cases: "I knew of only three among the thousand men who must have come and gone in those eight months. None of us blamed them or derided them—in fact I remember someone saying 'I wish I had the guts to go LMF,' and not entirely as a joke—but those three chaps were treated pretty harshly. They were sent away to some corrective establishment, they lost their rank and privileges, and their documents were labeled 'lack of moral fibre.' I expect the stigma stayed with them for life."

In the treatment of its weaker members, the RAF's posture was different from the USAAF's, which was less censorious and a great deal more humane: in the Eighth Air Force, "combat fatigue" was a condition to be recognized and treated with compassion. Larry Bird of the 493rd Bomb Group knew one crewman at Debach who decided, halfway through his second tour, that the time had come to stop. "His buddy was killed and he just wouldn't fly anymore. You never heard anybody say a word against him. Everybody was as friendly as they ever were." Tail gunner Paul Sink corroborated this: "I never heard of anyone who was mistreated or ostracized when he got to the point where he wouldn't fly anymore. They came into the mess hall like everyone else did. I had some good friends who got to that point, and I had a lot of sympathy with them because I knew what it was like."

The RAF practice, when a new crew joined a squadron, was to give the pilot his first experience of action by flying as "second dickey" with a seasoned crew, while his own men stayed behind, hoping they would see him back again. Some Eighth Air Force squadrons followed that procedure: on others the process of initiation was reversed. "What they did with a new crew," Bosshardt observed, "was to send them on their first mission with an experi-

enced co-pilot, while their own co-pilot went with another crew. Our first co-pilot was a guy named Leo Hipp from New Jersey. The plane he went in suffered some hits and had one or two engines out. In trying to land it at the base it got out of control, and Leo and all the crew but two were killed. That made us all superstitious about flying with anyone other than our own pilot."

"The crew was very congenial," said Paul Sink. "We were very close. If a person didn't meet the expectations of the rest of the crew, he was replaced. We took classes together and spent a lot of time together. When we weren't flying, we'd go to the tower and watch the group take off. Sometimes we'd split in half, and each group would do what they wanted to do, but most of the time we were nine people together. You got to know those people very well. After you flew missions with people, especially in combat, you got to know what their reaction would be in any given circumstance."

The more I work with the crew, the more satisfied I am that I've been extremely lucky. The way they take care of their guns and how anxious they are to learn makes me very happy. Wilhite and Twogood have been able to do something about most every mechanical trouble we've had. Every man can handle any turret. I believe our chances of coming through are good.
—Keith Newhouse, pilot, 467th Bomb Group, Eighth U.S. Army Air Force

When the Lord created man, he gave him two ends, one to sit on, and one to think with. Ever since that day man's success or failure has been dependent on the one he uses the most. It has always been, and is now, a case of heads you win and tails you lose.
—from Tee Emm

It never was and never could be a mode of warfare to be conducted in hot blood; the bomber crew was engaged throughout a flight in a series of intricate tasks . . . calculations and minute adjustments of machinery had to be made all the time with a clear head and a steady hand. To be a member of a bomber crew required persistent fortitude at a time when the stoutest mind and heart would have every excuse to show a natural and normal weakness. The average operation was in darkness and in the early hours of the morning; every one who took part in it knew that the odds were against the survival of any particular airman.
—W. J. Lawrence, historian of No. 5 Group, RAF Bomber Command

Quit yourselves like men.
—I Samuel 4:9

You can't slow up the formation for ten men in a crippled plane when it endangers the lives of hundreds more. The policy is to let the unfortunate drop out, so a fellow either rides the hell out of his remaining three engines and stays in, or peels off and takes a chance on getting a fighter escort back.
—Keith Newhouse, pilot, 467th Bomb Group, Eighth U.S. Army Air Force

A British Raid

Members of an RAF Stirling crew and their aircraft.

The story of Peenemünde begins in April 1943, when reports of unusual enemy activity on the Baltic coast reach the British government. The photo-recce of the peninsula shows newly-built laboratories, a living site, and areas that, after long consideration, the interpreters identify as missile-launching pads. It is known that German research into the atom bomb hads-made little progress, and that a massive effort is being put into the development of pilotless bombers and long-range rockets. In Winston Churchill's words, "Peenemünde is the summit of research and experiment."

Throughout the early summer, intelligence material about the "V-weapons" continues to accumulate. It reveals that Hitler intends to commence a bombardment of London on 30 October; by the end of the year, the Führer hopes, the city will be devastated, the British will give in, and, free of invasion threats against the western seaboard, the full weight of the Wehrmacht can be thrown against the Russians. The threat is a real one, and plans to evacuate the capital, wholly or partially, are taken from the shelf where they have lain dormant since 1939.

Meanwhile, Whitehall then decides that every effort must be made to put Peenemünde out of business, and the task, code-named Hydra (the many-headed snake that gave Hercules so much trouble), is assigned to Air Chief Marshal Harris. Instructions are issued from "the hole" at High Wycombe: the attack will be in strength, and in full moonlight, despite the advantage to the German fighters; the crews are not to know the nature of the target—only that this Hydra has to be eliminated, however herculean the task.

There are innovations: the bombing height band will be 8,000 to 10,000 feet—less than half the norm, a "master of ceremonies" will control events above the target for the first time in a full-scale attack, and new, slow-burnbing "spot fires" will be used as target markers. In the late afternoon of Tuesday 17 August, almost six hundred bomber crews assemble in briefing rooms throughout the length and breadth of eastern England.

One of those crews was that of Jack Currie. "We had come together in the usual random manner, responding to a call of 'Sort yourselves out, chaps,' in an echoing hangar at the operational training unit. Within five minutes, a bomber crew was formed: three bright Australians (the first I had met) as navigator, bomb-aimer, and rear gunner, a quiet Northumbrian as wireless operator, and me. Later, converting to the Lancaster, we had added two teenagers: a Welshman as mid-upper gunner and a Merseysider as flight engineer. At least I was no longer the youngest in the crew.

"We were assigned to No. 12 Squadron—'the shiny dozen'—at Wickenby, near Lincoln, and they seemed to need us: they had lost four crews in seven days. Ahead lay a tour of thirty operations, and the chances of survival were roughly one in four; they improved, said the old hands, if you got through five missions. We did that, and another three; now we were ready for our ninth.

"I had come to trust the aeroplane and to know the crew. Jim Cassidy, having quietly used a sick-bag as soon as we were airborne, would navigate us to Germany and back with no further trace of frailty. He had always set his heart on being a navigator, unlike many who first aspired to pilots' wings; he had come out top in training, and it showed. Larry Myring, to whom bloody was an all-purpose, mandatory adjective, would complain about the cold and be happy only when the target came in sight. The gunners Charlie Lanham and George Protheroe were always constantly alert; up to now, they had not been required to fire their

66

'Nick Kosciuk, a Polish bomber pilot, flew RAF Wellingtons in World War Two.

below: Running up the Merlin engines of an RAF Lancaster bomber prior to a raid; at bottom: Built mainly of wood, the ultra-fast de Havilland Mosquito was among the most impressive high-performance planes of the war years.

guns in anger. Charles Fairbairn would be heard only when something urgent—a recall, a diversion, or a change of wind—came through on the radio, and Johnny Walker would do what was needed to conserve the fuel. My responsibility, as captain, was to make the big decisions—like which dance hall or cinema we went to on a stand-down night.

"The Hydra briefing started with a little white lie. The enemy, said the intelligence officer, were developing a new generation of radar-controlled nightfighters on the Baltic coast. That was the carrot. The squadron commander took over with the stick. If we failed to clobber Peenemünde tonight, we would go again the next night and the next, until we did. The attack, he continued, would comprise three ten-minute waves: the first would hit the scientists' living quarters, the second wave the airfield (in reality, the rocket-launching sites), and the third the laboratories.

'Hey, Skip,' Myring whispered, 'what's our squadron motto?'

"I glanced at him. 'You know perfectly well.'

'Yeah. Leads The Field. So how is it we're always in the last bloody wave?'

"The PFF (Pathfinders) would employ the Newhaven method—which meant visual ground marking, and would re-centre the markers on each successive aiming point. We were to listen out on channel C for the MC's instructions and follow them to the letter. Purely as a precaution, in case the markers should be temporarily obscured, we were to approach the target on 'time-and-distance' runs from Cape Arkona on Rügen Island, forty miles north of Peenemünde. The outbound route would keep us clear of known flak concentrations, and the target defences were expected to be light. As for the enemy nightfighters, they would be diverted by no less than eight Mosquitoes bothering Berlin at the time of the attack.

"After the navigation leader had specified the courses, heights and airspeeds, the weatherman performed his magic-lantern show of cloud tops and bases. 'Looks good,' said Cassidy. 'Larry should get plenty of visual pinpoints.' He looked meaningfully at the bomb-aimer, whose map-reading ability he had sometimes questioned. Myring then grunted: for him, the main business of the briefing began only when the bombing leader took the stage. He licked his pencil, and made a careful note of how his five-ton load would be disposed.

"The signals leader spoke in an apologetic undertone: 'I would like to see all wireless operators for just a few minutes after briefing.' I leaned across to ask Fairbairn , 'What's all the secrecy, Charles? Why can't he tell everybody?'

'It's just technical stuff, Jack. A pilot wouldn't understand.'

"The veteran gunnery leader, with a battered service cap worn at an angle, advised constant vigilance. Defying popular belief, he saw the moonlight as being to our advantage: 'A fighter will stick out like a sore thumb,' he observed. 'Just keep your eyes peeled and make sure you see him before he sees you.'

"The station commander strolled onto the stage, one hand in his pocket, the other smoothing a sleek, dark moustache. He was sure he didn't have to emphasize the importance of the target, and anxious that there should be no early returns. 'Your flying meals will be ready at nineteen-thirty hours, transport to the aircraft at twenty-fifteen. Good luck, chaps.' to eliminate the swing by leading with the throttle of the port outer engine until the speed was high enough to get the rudders in the airflow for directional control. That was what I did at thirty minutes after nine, and PH-George 2 climbed away at maximum boost and 2,850 rpm. At fields all over Lincolnshire, in Yorkshire, and in East Anglia, 595 pilots did the same. Theoretically, if every aircraft stayed within a two-mile radius of base, their climbing orbits should never coincide: in practice, they occasionally did, and we took precautions. Apart from the navigator, busy at the gee box, every man kept watch.

"We reached 8,000 feet in under twenty minutes, and that was not too bad. Climbing in a circle wasted lift and thrust: aeroplanes climbed better in nice straight lines. When George 2 was straightened out on course she gained another 3,000 feet in the next five minutes. (It was a curious convention with aircraft, as with ships, that no matter how obviously masculine their names, they were always female to their crews.)

"Beneath us there was nothing to be seen: the coastal crossing point at Mablethorpe did not exist as houses, streets, and shoreline, but as 53.20N 00.16E on the navigator's chart. At two minutes before ten, I switched off the navigation lights and the IFF, and George 2 headed out across the unseen waters in a straight line for 'point A,' seventy miles west of the North Frisian Islands.

'Skipper from mid-upper, okay to test the guns?'

'Go ahead.'

"The Lancaster trembled as the gunners fired short bursts from their Brownings, and the sharp smell of cordite filtered through my mask. Climbing steadily, I followed the eternal visual routine: clockwise round the panel, clockwise round the sky. 'Cultivate the roving eye, Coo-ree,' were the words that First Lieutenant Sena, U.S. Army Air Corps, had constantly intoned when he was teaching me to fly the Vultee BT-13. Then, there were only 'needle, ball, and airspeed' and the clear blue sky of Georgia for the eye to rove around, but the principle held good. "I leveled out at 18,000 feet, and Walker brought the pitch back to cruising rpm.

below: Crossing the threshhold of its English base, an Avro Lancaster bomber returns from a night raid on a German target; right: An RAF bomber crew dressing for action.

George 2 reached point A at twenty minutes after eleven. 'Pilot from navigator, turn onto one-zero-seven magnetic.'

'One-zero-seven, turning on.'

'I'm losing the gee signals now, but I think we're pretty well on track.'

"I conjured up a mental map of the Frisian Islands. 'Let's try not to overfly Sylt, Jim.'

'No, she'll be right, Jack. We should be well north of it.'

"Someone switched a mike on. With two of the crew, I knew who it was before he spoke: Myring, because his mask never seemed to keep the slipstream noises out, and Fairbairn, because he always gave two low whistles—phsew, phsew—to check that he had switched from radio to intercom. This was Myring. 'Can't we have the bloody heat up a bit? It's cold enough down here to freeze the balls off a brass bloody monkey.'

"I said, 'No chatter, Larry,' but I had to admit he had a point. The aircraft's fabric wore a ghostly film of frost: ice crystals sparkled on the aerials and guns. I was beating alternate hands on knees to retain some sense of touch, and was starting to lose contact with my feet.

'Wireless op, is the cabin heat on full?'

Cassidy answered for him. 'He's on WT, listening out for the group broadcast.'

'Tell him to turn the heat up when he's finished.'

Aw, it's pretty well up now, Jack.'

'Not enough. The outside air temperature is less than minus twenty.'

"It was all right for Fairbairn. He sat nearest to the hot air vent. He could have flown in his underwear if he didn't have to move around the aircraft now and then. Cassidy was all right too: his navigation desk, forward of the wireless set, was never really cold. Walker and I

left: Fueling a Lancaster; below: Inspecting an outboard engine of a Short Stirling; bottom left: Tea break for this returned Halifax crew; bottom centre: A Lancaster pilot and and his engineer; bottom right: A Halifax crew after an op.

further forward in the cabin, were only ever warm when we were flying at low altitude on a summer's day, and Myring's station in the nose was colder than a tax collector's heart.

'Pilot from navigator, enemy coast coming up in two minutes.'

'Roger. Let's have an intercom check. Bomb-aimer?'

'Loud and clear, Skip.'

'Wireless op?'

'Phsew, phsew. Strength five.'

'Mid-upper . . .'

"At eleven-fifteen, the moon showed its head above the northeastern horizon. Myring, mindful of the navigator's hint, came through on the intercom. 'Bomb-aimer, Jim. We're crossing the coast now—fairly well on track.'

'I need it exactly, Larry.'

'Oh yeah. Well, about fifteen miles south of Esbjerg, or whatever they call the bloody place.'

'Lat and long, Larry, and the time.'

'Christ, Jim. It's not that easy down here, trying to use me bloody torch an' look at the bloody map, and—'

"I cut in. 'Do your best, bomb-aimer.'

"As George 2 headed east-southeast across the southern plains of Denmark, "Lanham called from the rear turret: 'Flak astern of us, ten degrees to starboard.'

'Roger.' Some airmen behind us were a little south of track, and the guns of Sylt were making them aware of it.

"Walker checked the fuel. George 2 was half a ton lighter than her takeoff weight. 'Let's reduce the revs a bit,' I suggested. 'We should be able to maintain airspeed at twenty-three hundred.'

"Walker inched the levers down and I turned the elevator trim minutely back. George 2 reacted badly to the trivial economy. Her indicated airspeed fell by nearly five miles per hour, and she handled like a ship without a rudder.

'No go, Johnny. Try twenty-three-fifty.'

"Ten minutes passed while we struggled to regain George 2's goodwill. Five minutes before midnight, Myring came through with a pinpoint; ten minutes later he produced another. 'Fifty-four forty-eight north, twelve thirty-nine east, time . . . er, bloody hell . . . zero-zero-zero-five.'

'Good on yer, Larry,' said Cassidy.

"I began a gradual descent to the bombing height as George 2 crossed the southern Swedish islands and continued east-southeast. The moonlight showed the shapes of other bombers, well scattered, moving like a ghostly skein of geese across the Baltic Sea. 'The wind's picked up a bit,' said the navigator. 'We'll be early at point C. Can you reduce the speed?'

'Can't go much slower than one-fifty, Jim. I can make an orbit. How much time do you want to lose?'

'Three minutes ought to do it.'

"It was not a maneuver I would have cared to make in total darkness or in cloud but, in the moonlight, it was not too hazardous. While the crew watched out, George 2 completed a wide descending circle without bumping into any other aeroplanes. Shortly before we reached the turning point at Cape Arkona, Myring saw the first green spot fires burning on Peenemünde. The time was seventeen minutes after midnight, and we had fifty miles to run.

"The last wind velocity Cassidy had found was from 290 degrees at forty miles per hour; Myring fed the numbers into the bombsight's calculator. Now the curve of the coast was perfectly distinct, and a white line of surf showed on the shore. The scene ahead was much less serene. The detonating 'cookies' made bright, expanding circles, like heavy stones dropped into pools of liquid fire; searchlights were waving, flak bursts were twinkling, and fires were taking hold. Not so many searchlights, nor so much flak as we were accustomed to, but a lot of smoke—more than the fires would seem to justify. The people on Peenemünde were putting up a smoke screen. It was a nice try, and it might have been successful—if the wind hadn't blown it out to sea.

"From 9,000 feet, in the light of the full moon, the target was much closer, and warmer, than the norm. I told Fairbairn to reduce the cabin heat, and Walker turned the oxygen to 'high.' On the starboard beam an interlacing pattern of tracer bullets appeared and disappeared. The voice of the MC sounded on the radio, the cool, clear voice of someone accustomed to command. It was strange, and rather comforting, to hear that English voice on the headphones, high above the Baltic, six hundred miles from home. 'Come in, third wave, and bomb the centre of the green Tis. Let's have a good concentration. Aim right at the centre of the greens.'

'Switches on,' said Myring, in the special, growling tone he adopted for the moment—his moment of all moments. 'Bombs fused and selected.'

"I took a deep breath and a fresh grip on the wheel. A spatter of light flak danced around George 2: I tried to pretend it wasn't there. 'Running in nicely, Skip,' said Myring, 'steady as she goes.'

'Third wave, don't bomb short. Make sure you aim at the centre of the greens.' I turned down the volume; from now on Myring was in charge.

'Bomb doors open, Skip.'

"I pushed the lever. The roar of the slipstream made a deeper sound as the bomb bay gaped. George 2 tried to raise her nose, and I stilled her with the trim tab. 'Lanc on fire at four o'clock level,' said Lanham. 'It's going down.'

'Steady,' Myring growled, 'left . . . left . . . steady . . . a touch left, and steady . . . steady . . . bombs gone!'

"Down went the 4,000-pound cookie, six 1,000-pounders and the two 500-pounders. George 2 lifted as they fell. Cassidy logged the time: thirty-eight minutes after midnight. 'Bomb doors closed,' called Myring. 'Steady for the camera.' In the last few minutes he had uttered thirty words without a single bloody. He really was a changed man with a bomb-tit in his hand.

'Bomb doors closed,' I echoed, pulling up the lever and rolling back the trim. Thirty seconds passed while the photo plates ticked over, and before I turned George 2 away, away from the brightly burning debris that was Peenemünde. 'New course, nav?'

'Two-nine-five degrees magnetic.'

'Turning on. Give me twenty-eight-fifty, Johnny, and we'll grab some altitude.'

"George 2 climbed away smoothly and headed to the west. We had no way of knowing that the Nachtjagd controllers, aware now that the Berlin raid was no more than a feint, had redirected all their available Messerschmitts and Junkers to our homeward route.

"The Lancaster's electronics included a receiver that picked up transmissions from the

below: Fueling and bombing-up
a Short Stirling.

Lichtenstein radar sets in the German fighters. The radar device was code-named Boozer, perhaps because the red lamp it lighted on the panel was reminiscent of a heavy drinker's nose. At 18,000 feet over Stralsund, thirty miles west of Peenemünde, the roving eye picked the glow up straight away.

'Rear gunner from pilot, I have a Boozer warning.'

'Rear gunner watching out astern.'

"Boozer also read transmissions from the ground-based Würzburg radars, which could be quite a nuisance when you were flying in the stream; at all times, however, you had to heed the signal. It was as well we did: seconds later, Lanham spoke again. 'Fighter at seven o'clock low. Stand by to corkscrew.'

'Standing by.'

'Mid-upper from rear gunner. There could be a pair. I'll take care of this one, you watch out.'

"I didn't like the sound of that remark. It would be difficult enough to evade one fighter in the moonlight, let alone two. I sat up straight, and gently shook the wheel. Don't get excited, George 2, but you might be doing some aerobatics any minute now.

'Prepare to corkscrew port, Jack . . . corkscrew port . . . go!'

'Going port.'

"I used heavy left aileron and rudder, elevators down, held the diving turn through fifteen degrees. I pulled out sharply and turned hard to starboard halfway through a climb. George 2 responded like a PT-17—a PT-17 weighing twenty-five tons.

'Foxed him, Jack. He's holding off, level on the starboard quarter.'

"Protheroe then came through. 'Another bandit, Skipper, four o'clock high, six hundred yards. It's an Me 210 . . .'

"Lanham broke in. 'Watch him, George, here comes number one again. Corkscrew starboard . . . go!'

"According to the navigator's log, the combat continued for another eight minutes: to me it seemed longer. After each frustrated pass, the attacker held off, content to occupy the attention of one gunner, while his partner came on in. I longed to have the heat turned down—the sweat was running down my face—but I dared not interrupt the gunners' running commentary. The sound of heavy breathing was sufficiently distracting, and I knew that it was mine.

"My wrists and forearms were reasonably strong, but I was no Charles Atlas, and George 2 wasn't feeling like a Stearman anymore. It occurred to me that these two fighter pilots were just playing games with us, biding their time until I was exhausted. Then they would rip the Lancaster to shreds. The sheet of armour plate behind me seemed pitifully small and there was a lot of me it failed to shield. If only our Brownings had a greater range; if only I could find a layer of cloud to hide in; if only the moonlight wasn't quite so bright . . .

'Corkscrew port . . . go!'

"Throwing George 2 into another diving turn, I looked back through the window. There was the Messerschmitt again, turning steeply with me as the pilot tried to bring his guns to bear. I could see his helmet and his goggles, looking straight at me. Staring back at him, I felt a sudden surge of anger, and a change of mood. You're not good enough, Jerry, I thought, to win this little fight. You're a bloody awful pilot and a damn poor shot. 'Well, for Christ's sake,

Punting on the Cam in the heart of bomber country; right: The Flying Control tower at the Tholthorpe Halifax base in Yorkshire; below: A memory of the spartan life in a Nissen hut; bottom right: Other memories, smoked on the ceiling of the Eagle pub in Cambridge.

Lancaster aircrew, above, a wireless operator;
right: A bomb-aimer.

George,' I squawked into the microphone, 'shoot that bastard down.'

"Instantly, the Lancaster vibrated. At first the flashes dazzled me, but when Protheroe fired a second burst I saw the streams of tracer make a sunbright parabola between George 2 and the fighter's nose. The Messerschmitt rolled over and went down. The last I saw of that bloody awful pilot was a long trail of smoke, ending in the stratus far below.

'I think you got him,' I said. 'Where's the other one?'

'Falling back astern,' said Lanham. 'He's clearing off. Probably out of ammo or fuel.'

'Good shooting, George. What kept you?'

'Sorry, Skipper. I had my sights on him all the time. I guess I just forgot to pull the trigger.'

'Pilot from nav, let me know when you're back on course.'

'Roger.'

'Bomb-aimer, Skip. I was ready for the buggers, but they never came in bloody range of the front bloody guns.'

"Larry was himself again. I checked the compass and turned toward the coast of Lübeck Bay. I was thinking of the Welshman sitting in the turret with the fighter in his sights. He had fired a lot of rounds on training ranges and at air-towed target drogues, but he had never fired a bullet at another human being. That was rather different, and I thought I understood why he had needed the command to open fire.

'Nav from pilot, back on course. Let's all settle down.'

"I held the wheel loosely and stroked the rudder pedal with the balls of my feet. George 2 was flying head-on into wind and her speed across the water was a mere 176 mph. It was going to be a long ride back to Wickenby, but I believed that we would make it. At twenty minutes after one, Lanham reported in that the Peenemünde fires could still be seen.

Forty-three minutes later, a searchlight reared ahead, pale in the moonlight but no less dangerous for that. I really hated searchlights. Over the target, you just had to ignore them, but I did my best to dodge them when we were on our own. If that master beam latched on, its two slaves would quickly follow, and few aircraft, once coned, returned to base unscathed. On the way home from Hamburg two weeks earlier, we had got away with it—more by luck than good judgment. I didn't want to try our luck again. 'Going ten degrees starboard for two minutes, Jim.' The beam waved toward us, like a finger feeling for a keyhole in the dark; it groped for a while and then disappeared. Back on course, George 2 began her second crossing of the cold North Sea.

"Just after three o'clock, the gee box showed its first good signals since she faded at point A four hours ago. Cassidy plotted the position. For close on a thousand miles, by dead reckoning, a bearing on Polaris, and three or four pinpoints, he had navigated George 2 to within a mile of where she ought to be. He gave no sign of being surprised. 'Pilot from nav, we're pretty well on track. ETA base is zero-four-zero-five.'

"Walker reduced the rpm. The vertical speed indicator showed a descent rate of three hundred feet a minute: if I maintained that flight path, we should arrive over Wickenby more or less at circuit height and all set for a landing. Provided, of course, that I remembered to lower the undercarriage, nothing then could keep us from breakfast or from bed. Not that the gunners could relax: there could be no worse anti-climax than to get chopped by an intruder in the airfield circuit.

'Pilot to crew, we're below oxygen height. Smoke if you can afford it.'

"At about four o'clock, the Mablethorpe searchlight stood erect, the only searchlight I was ever glad to see. I switched on the navigation lights and the IFF, and Fairbairn stood ready with the colours of the day. Ten minutes later, a beacon twinkled dead ahead. It read 'dit-dit-dah-dah-dit-dit'—the code for Wickenby. I told Walker to turn the oxygen up to the 20,000-feet level, and pushed the RT button 'A.' 'Hello, Orand, this is Nemo George 2, are you receiving me, over?'

'Hello, Nemo George 2, this is Orand. Receiving you loud and clear, over.'

'Orand, George 2 approaching from the east, fifteen-hundred feet. Permission to join the circuit, over.'

'George 2, the circuit is busy. You're clear to join at four thousand and stand by. Left-hand orbit, two aircraft at that height, over.'

'Shit,' said Walker, 'we're in the flipping stack.'

'Yeah,' snarled Myring, 'that's the bloody snag with being in the last bloody wave.'

'Shut up,' I counseled. 'It's a lovely night for flying. Twenty-eight-fifty rpm, engineer.'

"For the next thirty minutes, George 2 orbited the beacon, gradually descending in five-hundred-foot stages at Orand's command. Later in the tour, I would learn to take some shortcuts, to make a better speed, and to arrive at Wickenby before the stack began, but in those days, a green sergeant pilot, I didn't know the score. At last the call came through: 'George 2, you're cleared to one thousand feet and number two to land. Runway two-seven, Queenie Fox Easy one-zero-one-two. Call downwind, over.'

"I set the altimeter and began the landing drill. 'Trailing aerial in, Charles. Brake pressure, Johnny? Fuel?'

'Plenty of both.'

'Rad shutters open. Check 'M' gear.'

"At one thousand feet, a mile south of the field, I turned parallel with the twin lines of the runway lights, and reduced the power.

Vickers Wellington bombers on a practice mission over England in WW2.

Orand, George 2 downwind, over.'

'George 2, you're clear to funnels, one ahead.'

'Wheels down, Johnny.'

''The undercarriage lamps shone red as the uplocks disengaged, and the nose dropped a fraction as the airflow hit the wheels. The locks engaged with a jolt, and the lamps turned to green. 'Flap fifteen. Booster pumps on.'

''When the last set of lights at the runway's downwind end were level with the port wingtip, I brought the airspeed back to 140 and turned toward the field. Halfway through the turn, the funnel lights on the port quarter beckoned like the gates of home. As the nose swing into line, I inched the throttles back and let Sir Isaac Newton do his stuff. 'George 2 funnels, over.'

'George 2, you're clear to land. Wind is eighteen degrees from your right at ten knots, over.'

'Half flap, Johhny. Pitch fully fine.'

''I held the nose down to counteract the lift and steered a mite to starboard to compensate for drift. The lights of the runway seemed to widen at the threshold and to taper in the distance up ahead. 'Full flap. Stand by for landing.'

''As George 2 crabbed across the threshold, Walker held the throttles back against the stops, I kicked the nose straight and pulled the wheel into my lap. The tyres squealed on the tarmac at 04:49.''

The record showed that 560 aircraft reached the target and dropped 1,800 tons of bombs, 85 per cent of which were high explosive. When the truth was revealed about the Baltic base, it was said that Hydra set the V-weapon programme back by several months and reduced the scale of the eventual attack. Certainly, no flying bombs fell on England until June 1944, and no rockets until the following September. General Dwight D. Eisenhower was to write later: ''If the Germans had succeeded in perfecting and using these new weapons six months earlier our invasion of Europe would have proved exceedingly difficult, perhaps impossible.''

One hundred and eighty Germans, mostly scientists and technicians, died in the attack, and General Jeschonnek, the Luftwaffe Chief of Staff, gave proof of his dismay by committing suicide the next day. Sadly, the first Newhaven markers went down on the camp where the slave workers were sleeping, and over five hundred unhappy lives were lost.

The Nachtjagd, it transpired, had deployed a new device: twin, upward-firing cannons, mounted behind the cockpit of the Me110s and fired by the pilot with the aid of a reflector sight, enabled the fighter crew to attack the bomber's blind spot underneath the fuselage. This deadly piece of weaponry, known as Schräge Musik, was believed to have inflicted some of the losses suffered on the night: twenty-three Lancasters, fifteen Halifaxes, two Stirlings, and one of the Mosquitoes.

For the future, an airborne MC or master bomber (the role of ''Honest John'' Searby, 83 Squadron's commander, over Peenemünde), would control all major raids, and the innovative tactics for re-centering ground markers were to be retained.

Peenemünde would be the target for three Eighth Air Force missions in July and August 1944, but Hydra was, and would remain, the RAF's only full-scale precision attack in the last two years of the war.

Knowing nothing of these matters, we drank our cocoa with a tot of rum and attended the debriefing. The crew were in good spirits: we had hit a vital target, dodged the searchlights and the flak, outflown one Messerschmitt and destroyed another—well, possibly destroyed. It seemed a shame to remind them, as we ate our eggs and bacon, that we hadn't yet completed one-third of our tour.

We're on ops tonight. Target Munich . . . Quite naturally we're all very tired and moaning because it will be another trip of eight hours . . . a spoonful of pink mixture to settle my stomach, five BI tablets to give me a bit of energy and two caffeine tablets to keep me awake, so I felt like a walking chemist's shop.
—from *Journeys Into Night* by Don Charlwood

I have taught you my dear flock, for above thirty years how to live; and I will show you in a very short time how to die.
—Sandys

Having released its bombs, each aircraft was supposed to continue on the same steady course with bomb doors open until a photograph of the result was obtained. The camera in the bomb bay was triggered by flares released with the bombs. Good target photographs were not too common. The camera could be prematurely triggered by someone else's flares.

The ugliest of trades have their moments of pleasure. Now, if I were a grave-digger, or even a hangman, there are some people I could work for with a great deal of enjoyment.
—from *Ugly Trades* by Douglas Jerrold

We were going out in daylight. Three hundred and fifty on the raid. The bomb-aimer was up front looking out. He said, 'Enemy coast coming up . . . now.' The navigtor said, 'Bang on time.' I'm sitting at the back and I said, 'In that case there's three hundred and forty-nine other buggers late, 'cause I can see them fifty miles behind us.' I'd no sooner said that than 'boom, boom,' and the shells burst just behind me. They were getting closer. I said, 'Dive port,' and the skipper turned and dived straight away. Just as well, because the next one burst exactly where I'd been. It blew the perspex off the turret. Cut me eye and me thumb a bit as well.
—Fred Allen, rear gunner, 158 Squadron, RAF Bomber Command

Germany heard a clashing of arms all over the sky; the Alps trembled with uncommon earthquakes. Never did lightnings fall in greater quantity from a serene sky, or dire thunders blaze so often.
—from *Georgics* by Virgil

You may be interested to know that the flak guns in Berlin are being fired by fifteen-year-old boys as fast as Russian prisoners of war can load them.
—Briefing officer, RAF Wickenby, November 1943

e bomber escort fighters flown
the Eighth Air Force in the
ond World War included, above,
Republic P-47 Thunderbolt; the
ckheed P-38 Lightning, at right,
the North American P-51
stang, left, the only Allied fighter
able of shepherding the daylight
mbers of the Eighth to the deep-
German targets and back to
r bases in England.

A spectacular image of Flying Fortress bombers of the 390th Bomb Group, 8AF, together with their 'little friends,' the escort fighters that protected them from attack by enemy fighters during the hazardous raids of the Anglo-American combined bombing offensive in the European air war.

below: A P-47 Thunderbolt on its hardstand at its 56th Fighter Group base in England.

Bomber escorts. far left: 4FG commander Colonel Don Blakeslee; centre: Captain William O'Brien, 357th Fighter Group; below, in cockpit: Captain Walker Mahurin,

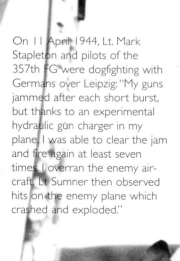

On 11 April 1944, Lt. Mark Stapleton and pilots of the 357th FG were dogfighting with Germans over Leipzig: "My guns jammed after each short burst, but thanks to an experimental hydraulic gun charger in my plane, I was able to clear the jam and fire again at least seven times. I overran the enemy aircraft. Lt Sumner then observed hits on the enemy plane which crashed and exploded."

Lt. Col. Francis Gabreski achieved twenty-eight aerial victories while with the 56th Fighter Group in England during World War Two. In the Korean War he was credited with a further 6.5 kills.

Captain John B. England, 357th FG, emerging from the cockpit of *Nooky Booky IV*, his P-51D Mustang fighter; bottom left: Captain Don Gentile of the 4FG; bottom right: Captain Jack Ilfrey of the 20FG at Kingscliffe.

99

below: American Mustang pilots just back from an 8AF escort mission:; bottom: An American P-38 Lightning pilot in his cockpit; right: Aces of the 56FG, left to right: Bob Johnson, Hub Zemke, and Bud Mahurin.

In recent years, parachuting has become a popular activity. From all sorts of altitudes, to free fall or with static lines, in teams or individually, people jump out of airplanes for fun. But jumping out because you had to—because there was no alternative—was never any fun. In the great air offensive of World War Two, many thousands of young men took that obligatory step into the sky, trusting slender silk and fiber to bear them safely down. And that was only the start of their adventure: there were no clubmates applauding the descent, no friendly sponsor offering a prize, but an alien environment, with the enemy in charge, and perhaps a population who bore them no goodwill. Their duty, they were told, lay in evasion and escape: bury your parachute, remove all distinguishing badges, lie low in daylight, and travel by night; make contact with the underground, try to reach a neutral country, find your way back to your squadron, and resume the fight . . .

Although the 379th Bomb Group lost fifteen B-17s in its first month of combat, it went on to fly more sorties, drop more bombs on target, and have fewer turn-backs than any other bomb group in the Eighth. The fact that it also had more cases of venereal disease suggests that the group pursued pleasure as vigourously as business, if rather less selectively. On 16 August 1943, a day before the first historic Schweinfurt raid, twenty-one aircraft of the 379th took part in an attack on a fighter airfield at Le Bourget. Albert Tyler, a twenty-nine-year-old from California, was flying his fourteenth mission as top turret gunner and flight engineer. The crew's regular pilot had recently been killed, and this was to be the co-pilot's first combat mission in command.

The formation was flying in the height band between 26,000 and 28,000 feet when the German fighters came at it head-on. Tyler never blamed the pilot for what happened next: "He was a hellova nice guy and we all liked him, but I guess he panicked. He did a real no-no. He pulled back on the stick and drove right up. We were on our own up there, with no protection from the other B-17s. We were a sitting duck."

Methodically, pairs of the fighters destroyed the lone aircraft, raking it with cannon fire from nose to tail. In the cabin, the hydraulic reservoir exploded, and some of the shattered metal lodged in Tyler's leg. The oxygen bottles were the next to go. Combustion quickly followed and the cabin filled with flame. The canvas cover of Tyler's parachute was burning as he clipped it on his harness. Observing that the pilot and co-pilot had already left the airplane (another no-no), Tyler took it on himself to give the order to abandon, and helped the bombardier and navigator to make their escape.

"I went out of the open bomb bay doors. Jumping from that height, I should have delayed pulling the ripcord, but I didn't want to take a chance on the chute catching fire, so I pulled it immediately. I passed out from lack of oxygen, but it could only have been seconds before I came to again."

Two Fw190s made passes as Tyler floated down and, at a lower altitude, an Me109 banked vertically around him. Tyler put his hand up in a gesture of salute; the enemy pilot did the same. Below him, he saw a stretch of forest and the river Oise; in the fields between were German trucks and soldiers. He was a good swimmer, and he tried to steer his chute toward the water, but in common with most airmen he had received no training in maneuvering a parachute. "I pulled the lines the wrong way, and I ended up in the tallest tree, right on the banks of the river. There were no Germans down there that I could see. In fact, I didn't see anybody for a while. Then a dog started barking, and a group of people gathered under the

Abandon!

above right: Sergeant Albert Tyler

The last moments of a Flying Fortress, shot down in flames over continental Europe.

tree. With my leg the way it was, I couldn't get down."

Once they were convinced that Tyler was American, the Frenchmen dispersed, taking a fallen flying boot as a souvenir. Then a sturdy youth, whom Tyler came to know as André, climbed the tree, half held and half dropped the airman to the ground, and concealed him in a pile of rocks. A few hours later, Tyler heard someone whistling "Yankee Doodle," and two small children came through the forest carrying a basket of bread, cheese, wine, and fruit. Having improvised a crutch, André found garments suited to the role of a peasant which Tyler, for the moment, would adopt.

That night, resting in a hayloft, they heard shouts of "Achtung, achtung," as German soldiers searched the neighbourhood. Next morning, they moved to a cave beside the river, where they were joined by one of Tyler's crew, escorted by the village mayor. Tyler was troubled: "Johnny was not our regular bombardier, and he was a very uncooperative guy. I thought he would be a real danger to me."

After the aimen had spent three nervous days in the cave, André returned with rail tickets for Paris. Although the train was thronged with soldiers, they paid no attention to the Americans, and Tyler was not called upon to use the deaf-and-dumb act he had rehearsed with André. In the Gare du Nord's urinal, Tyler and Johnny exchanged a word or two in English. "A German officer came out of the cubicle," said Tyler, "and put a pistol up against my kidneys. André hadn't said a word. He came over and jammed a hunting knife into the German's back. He said 'Allez, allez,' and we left in a hurry."

André took his charges to the apartment of a doughty female member of the French Resistance. "There was a big, open courtyard, and our bedrooms were right off a balcony that went round the house. Madame gave us everything we wanted to eat and drink. At the same time she was hiding and feeding a bunch of escaped French POWs. A very brave lady."

Meanwhile, the Resistance were planning the next move, which was almost a disaster. In a Paris suburb, they had to jump from a window in the middle of the night to evade a German search party. Their next port of call was a fine town house a mile or two from the Eiffel Tower, and the two weeks they spent there were the high spot of their stay in France.

"Every day," said Tyler, "Juliette surprised us with something—a duck, a lobster, and I mean a big one. It was very enjoyable. Her husband got a big kick taking us for a stroll around the sidewalk cafés in the afternoon. The trouble was that when the Germans saw Johnny's blond hair, they thought he was one of them, and tried to strike up a conversation. He could have been picked up real quick. I suggested shoe polish, but he didn't want his hair blacked. That guy fought us tooth and nail. I had to hold him down."

They accompanied Marcel, a saboteur, on a journey north of Paris, and watched him lay explosives on a railway line that carried German traffic. Later, they saw him choke a German sentry with a length of piano wire. "He wanted us," said Tyler, "to tell the English what the French Resistance were doing to help themselves."

Two days before the time came to move on, they saw barrage balloons rising over Paris, and watched from Juliette's patio while B-17s bombed the Renault engine plant across the Seine. On the train to central France, they were escorted by a priest. Arriving in Ville, they were welcomed by the mayor, who promptly threw a party. The whole town attended, much champagne was drunk, and Albert Tyler, not America's most accomplished pianist, played the "Marseillaise" fortissimo until the more cautious townsmen persuaded him to stop.

Their next stay was at a castle on a hilltop where, over a bottle of Jack Daniel's, they discovered that their host, having made an illicit booze fortune in the States, was making amends to society by collecting starving children from the poorer parts of Paris and fattening them on the products of his land. "He and his beautiful wife," said Tyler, "would take them back to town and pick up another load. That guy was some character."

Their priestly guide then left them, with instructions to take a certain train to Toulouse. In the compartment, Tyler's deaf-and-dumb act was successful until a stout lady, in rising to depart, happened to tread upon his foot. Tyler yelped, "Oh, shit," at which two Frenchmen got up from their seats, muttering "Allez, allez," and hustled the Americans away.

They were taken to a farmhouse below the northern foothills of the towering Pyrenees. That afternoon, with twenty more evaders and a guide, they set out to make a crossing into Spain. On the third day of the journey, they were halted by a blizzard, and their guide decamped, not only with his fee but with the party's store of food. While some men elected to continue on their own, Tyler and Johnny returned to the farmhouse for reprovisioning. Their next attempt to reach a neutral haven was eventually successful, but not without hardships.

"We were eating leaves and grass," said Tyler, "to supplement our rations. I ended up with a diarrhea you wouldn't believe. And they told me, 'We can't stop, we have to go on.' The Germans were patrolling those mountain trails with light aircraft."

"NO ENEMY PLANE WILL FLY OVER THE REICH TERRITORY"
HERMANN GOERING

S-Sugar is the oldest surviving Lancaster in the world,—delivered to the RAF in 1942,

'Cookies' being delivered to Lancasters on this RAF air base in England.

American newsman and war correspondent Edward R. Murrow recounted a bombing raid on which he flew with the crew of a Royal Air Force Lancaster on 4 December 1943: Last night, some of the young gentlemen of the RAF took me to Berlin. The pilot was called Jock. The crew captains walked into the briefing room, looked at the maps and charts and sat down with their big celluloid pads on their knees. The atmosphere was that of a school and a church. The pilots were reminded that Berlin is Germany's greatest center of war production. The intelligence officer told us how many heavy and light ack-ack guns; how many searchlights we might expect to encounter. Then, Jock, the wing commander, explained the system of marking, the kind of flares that would be used by the pathfinders. He said that concentration was the secret of success in these raids; that as long as the aircraft stayed well bunched, they would protect each other. The captains of aircraft walked out. I noticed that the big Canadian with the slow, easy grin had printed Berlin at the top of his pad and then embellished it with a scroll. The red-headed English boy with the two-weeks'-old mustache was the last to leave the room.

Late in the afternoon we went to the locker room to draw parachutes, Mae Wests and all the rest. As we dressed a couple of Australians were whistling. Walking out to the bus that was to take us to the aircraft, I heard the station loudspeakers announcing that that evening all personnel would be able to see a film: *Star-Spangled Rhythm*. Free.

We went out and stood around the big, black four-motored Lancaster, D for Dog. A small station wagon delivered a thermos bottle of coffee, chewing gum, an orange and a bit of chocolate for each man. Up in that part of England the air hums and throbs with the sound of aircraft motors all day, but for half an hour before takeoff, the skies are dead, silent and expectant. A lone hawk hovered over the airfield, absolutely still as he faced into the wind. Jack, the tail gunner, said, 'It'd be nice to fly like that,' D-Dog eased around the perimeter track to the end of the runway. We sat there for a moment. The green light flashed and we were rolling . . . ten seconds ahead of schedule.

The takeoff was as smooth as silk. The wheels came up and D-Dog started the long climb. As we came up through the clouds I looked right and left and counted fourteen black Lancasters climbing for the place where men must burn oxygen to live. The sun was going down and its red glow made rivers and lakes of fire on the top of the clouds. Down to the southward, the clouds piled up to form castles, battlements and whole cities, all tinged with red.

Soon we were out over the North Sea. Dave, the navigator, asked Jock if he couldn't make a little more speed. We were nearly two minutes late. By this time, we were all using oxygen. The talk on the intercom was brief and crisp. Everyone sounded relaxed. For a while, the eight of us, in our little world of exile, moved over the sea. There was a quarter moon on the starboard beam and Jock's quiet voice came through the intercom, 'That'll be flak ahead.' We were approaching the enemy coast. The flak looked like a cigarette lighter in a dark room: one that won't light—sparks but no flame—the sparks crackling just below the level of the cloud tops.

We flew steady and straight and soon the flak was directly below us. D-Dog rocked a little from right to left but that wasn't caused by the flak. We were in the slipstream of other Lancasters ahead and we were over the enemy coast.

Then a strange thing happened. The aircraft seemed to grow smaller. Jack, in the rear turret, Wally the mid-upper gunner, Titch the wireless operator, all seemed somehow to draw closer to Jock in the cockpit. It was as though each man's shoulder was against the others. The understanding was complete. The intercom came to life and Jock said, 'Two aircraft on the port beam.' Jack in the tail said, 'Okay, sir, they're Lancs.' The whole crew was a unit and wasn't wasting words. The cloud below was ten-tenths. The blue-green jet of the exhausts licked back along the wing and there were other aircraft all around us. The whole great aerial armada was hurtling toward Berlin.

We flew so for twenty minutes, when Jock looking up at a vapor trail curling above us, remarking in a conversational tone that, from the look of it, he thought there was a fighter on up there. Occasionally the angry red of the ack-ack burst through the clouds, but it was far away and we took only an academic interest. We were flying in the third wave.

Jock asked Wally in the mid-upper turret, and Jack in the rear, if they were cold. They said they were all right and thanked him for asking. He even asked how I was and I said, 'All right so far.' The cloud was beginning to thin out. Off to the north we could see lights and the flak began to liven up ahead of us. Buzz, the bomb-aimer crackled through on the intercom, 'There's a battle going on over on the starboard beam.' We couldn't see the aircraft but we could see the jets of red tracer being exchanged. Suddenly, there was a burst of yellow flame and Jock remarked, 'That's the fighter going down. Note the position.' The whole thing was interesting, but remote. Dave, the navigator, who was sitting back with his maps, charts and compasses, said, 'The attack ought to begin in exactly two minutes.' We were still over the clouds.

But suddenly those dirty gray clouds turned white and we were over the outer searchlight defenses. The clouds below us were white and we were black. D-Dog seemed like a black bug on a white sheet. The flak began coming up, but none if it close. We were still a long way from Berlin. I didn't realize just how far. Jock observed, 'There's a kite on fire dead ahead.' It was a great, golden, slow-moving meteor slanting toward the earth. By this time we were about thirty miles from our target area in Berlin. That thirty miles was the longest flight I have ever made.

Dead on time, Buzz the bomb-aimer reported. 'Target indicators going down.' At the same moment, the sky ahead was lit up by bright yellow flares. Off to starboard another kite went down in flames. The flares were sprouting all over the sky, reds and greens and yellows, and we were flying straight for the center of the fireworks. D-Dog seemed to be standing still, the four propellers thrashing the air, but we didn't seem to be closing in. The cloud had cleared and off to the starboard a Lanc was caught by at least fourteen searchlight beams. We could see him twist and turn and finally break out. But still the whole thing had a quality of unreality about it. No one seemed to be shooting at us, but it was getting lighter all the time. Suddenly, a tremendous big blob of yellow light appeared dead ahead; another to the right and another to the left. We were flying straight for them. Jock pointed out to me the dummy fires and flares looking like stoplights. Another Lanc was coned on our starboard beam. The lights seemed to be supporting it. Again we could see those little bubbles of colored lead driving at it **from** two sides. The German fighters were at him. And then, with no warning at all, D-Dog was filled with an unhealthy white light.

I was standing just behind Jock and could see all the seams on the wings. His quiet Scots

A Lancaster ready for takeoff.

some in our own ranks, countless others from your shores. To those who did not return the best memorial is the fellowship of our two countries, which by their valour they created and by their sacrifice they have preserved.
—Prime Minister Winston Churchill

He walked through the winding old streets of Archbury direct to a pub called the Black Swan, borrowed a bicycle from the bartender, slung his package to the handlebars and pedaled out of the village along a country road lined with hedges and shaggy houses with thatched roofs. Presently he turned off on a side road, propped his bike against a hedge and strode slowly a hundred yards out onto an enormous flat, unobstructed field. When he halted he was standing at the head of a wide, dilapidated avenue of concrete, which stretched in front of him with gentle undulations for a mile and a half. A herd of cows, nibbling at the tall grass which had grown up through the cracks, helped to camouflage his recollection of the huge runway. He noted the black streak left by tires, where they had struck the surface, smoking, and nearby, through the weeds which nearly covered it, he could still see the stains left by puddles of grease and black oil on one of the hard-stands evenly spaced around the five-mile circumference of the perimeter track, like teeth on a ring gear. And in the background he could make out a forlorn dark green control tower, surmounted by a tattered gray windsock and behind it two empty hangars, a shoe box of a water tank on high stilts and an ugly cluster of squat Nissen huts. Not a soul was visible, nothing moved save the cows, nor was there any sound to break the great quiet. A gust of wind blew back the tall weeds behind the hard-stand nearest him. But suddenly Stovall could no longer see the bent-back weeds through the quick tears that blurred his eyes and slid down the deep lines in his face. He made no move to brush them away. For behind the blur he could see, from within, more clearly. On each empty hard-stand there sat the ghost of a B-17, its four whirling propellers blasting the tall grass with the gale of its slip stream, its tires bulging under the weight of tons of bombs and tons of the gasoline needed for a deep penetration.
—from *Twelve O'Clock High* by Beirne Lay, Jr and Sy Bartlett

History is something that never happened, written by a man who wasn't there.
—anon

The last mission of a crew, and the relief of a safe return.

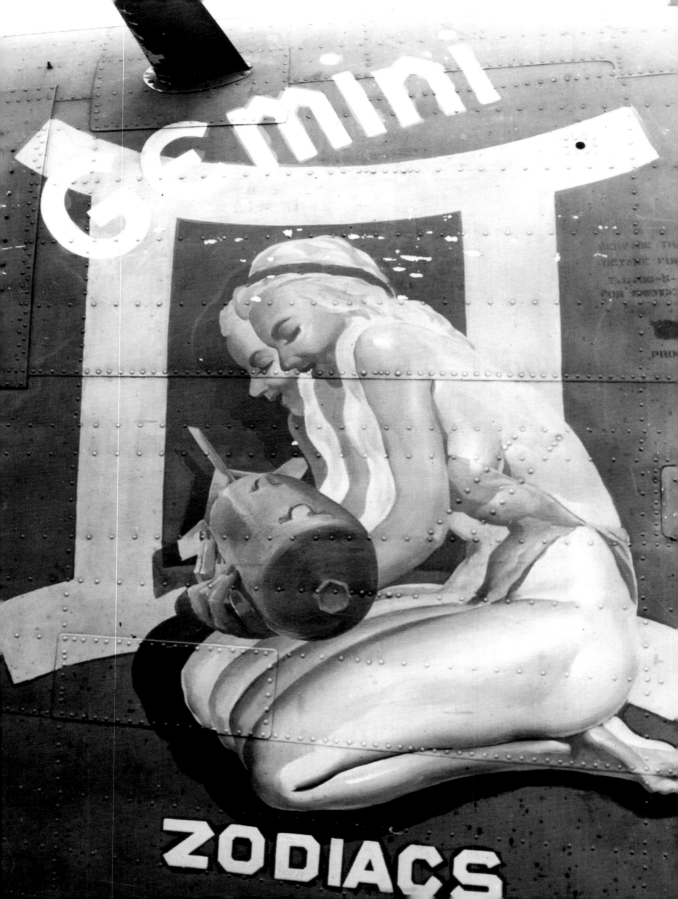

PICTURE CREDITS: PHOTOS FROM THE AUTHOR'S COLLECTION ARE CREDITED: AC; PHOTOS FROM THE U.S. NATIONAL ARCHIVES AND RECORDS ADMINISTRATION ARE CREDITED: NARA; PHOTOS FROM THE IMPERIAL WAR MUSEUM ARE CREDITED: IWM; P3-AC; P4-AC; P6-AC; P9-TOP: AC, BOTTOM: AC; P11 TOP-NARA, BOTTOM LEFT-AC, BOTTOM RIGHT-TONI FRISSELL/LIBRARY OF CONGRESS; P12 TOP-NARA, BOTTOM-AC; P13 TOP-NARA, BOTTOM-AC; P15 TOP-ASSOCIATED BRITISH PICTURES CORP, BOTTOM-AC; P16 TOP-AC, BOTTOM-AC; P17 TOP-AC, BOTTOM-AC; P19-AC; P20-NARA; P22-NARA; P25-NARA; P26-NARA; P28-AC; P29-NARA; P31-COLUMBIA PICTURES; P32-NARA; P34-TONI FRISSELL/LIBRARY OF CONGRESS; P36-QUENTIN BLAND; P39-USAF; P40-AC; P43-COLUMBIA PICTURES; P44-NARA; P45-KEITH NEWHOUSE; P46-AC; P47-NARA; P49-USAF ACADEMY; P51-TONI FRISSELL/LIBRARY OF CONGRESS; P52-AC; P53-AC; P54 BOTH-AC; P55 ALL-AC; P56 ALL-AC; P58-AC; P61-AC; P62-AC; P67-NICK KOSCIUK; P68 TOP-AC, BOTTOM-DE HAVILLAND; P70-AC; P71-AC; P72 BOTH-AC; P73 TOP-JONATHAN FALCONER, BOTTOM CENTRE-IWM, BOTTOM RIGHT-AC; P76-JONATHAN FALCONER; P78 BOTH-AC; P79 BOTH-AC; P80 BOTH-AC; P82-AC; P86-NARA; P88-AC; P89-AC; P90-USAF; P92 TOP-REPUBLIC AVIATION, BOTTOM-AC; P93-AC; P94-AC; P96 TOP LEFT-AC, TOP RIGHT-MERLE OLMSTED, BOTTOM-AC; P97 TOP-WALKER MAHURIN, BOTTOM-MERLE OLMSTED; P98-USAF ACADEMY; P99 TOP-MERLE OLMSTED, BOTTOM LEFT-AC, BOTTOM RIGHT-JACK ILFREY; P100 BOTH-AC; P101-AC; P103-ALBERT TYLER; P104-USAF ACADEMY; P106 TOP BOTH-AC, CENTRE AND BOTTOM-NARA; P109-NARA; P110-AC; P111-AC; P113 TOP LEFT-JONATHAN FALCONER, TOP RIGHT-USAF, BOTTOM-AC; P114-AC; P116-AC; P118-AC; P120-AC; P121-ASSOCIATED BRITISH PICTURES CORP; P123-AC; P124-NARA; P127 TOP LEFT-NARA, TOP RIGHT-TONI FRISSELL/LIBRARY OF CONGRESS, CENTRE AND BOTTOM LEFT-AC, BOTTOM RIGHT-ANDY SAUNDERS; P128 ALL-AC; P130-AC; P131-USAF ACADEMY; P133 BOTH-AC; P134-AC; P135 BOTH-AC; P136 BOTH-AC; P137 BOTH-AC; P138-AC; P139 ALL-AC; P140-AC; P141 BOTH-AC; P142 ALL-AC; P143 BOTH-AC; P144-QUENTIN BLAND.